D0220194

Giving My Body To Science

The Hugh MacLennan Poetry Series

Editors: Kerry McSweeney and Joan Harcourt
Selection Committee: Donald H. Akenson,
Philip Cercone, Allan Hepburn, and Carolyn Smart

giving my body to science

RACHEL ROSE

McGILL-QUEEN'S UNIVERSITY PRESS

Montreal & Kingston · London · Ithaca

© Rachel Rose 1999
ISBN 0-7735-1904-1

Legal deposit third quarter 1999
Bibliothèque nationale du Québec

Printed in Canada on acid-free paper
Reprinted 2004

McGill-Queen's University Press acknowledges the financial support
of the Government of Canada through the Book Publishing
Industry Development Program (BPIDP) for its activities.
We also acknowledge the support of the Canada Council
for the Arts for our publishing program.

Canadä

_____

Canadian Cataloguing in Publication Data

Rose, Rachel, 1970–
Giving my body to science
(The Hugh MacLennan poetry series)
ISBN 0-7735-1904-1
I. TITLE. II. SERIES.
PS8585.07325G59 1999   C811'.54   C99-900843-9
PR9199.3.R5884G59 1999

_____

This book was typeset
by Interscript
in 9.5/13 Baskerville.

for Isabelle

CONTENTS

ACKNOWLEDGMENTS

A special thanks to my father, James Prier, and my cousin, Herman Rose, for their generous financial support and for believing in my words. Thanks to Shelley Mason for sharing and encouraging my bibliophilia.

Thanks to Daphne Marlatt, Brian Garrett, Ellen Samuels, Lori McNulty and Carellin Brooks, for their careful and insightful editing and encouragement of my work. Thanks also to my writing group: Lia Barsotti, Frances Hahn, Susan Elmslie, and Masarah VanEyck, whose diverse talents continue to inspire and challenge.

Thanks to my parents, Robert and Mary Rose, for raising me in rooms filled with poetry, for reading me to sleep on William Blake and T.S. Eliot, for dragging me to interminable poetry readings as a child.

Thanks to Nathalie Cooke, mentor and friend.

Thanks to Carolyn Smart for her editing, her generosity, her friendship, and her steadfast encouragement.

Thanks to the Canada Council for the Explorations Grant.

Thanks to Kozo Takeuchi for the photograph and Sonia Chow for the design.

Thanks to Isabelle for providing a patient ear to the many midnight readings of fresh poems, for her clarity of voice, for sharing with me what goes on at the hospital, and for the daily joy she offers.

Giving My Body To Science

And if I say "tree"?
I'd say – death by wood.

Cabinet? *Casket.*
Tell me again.

A map. A map of the island
where I asked to be born.
            – Jeanne Marie Beaumont, *Rorschach*

For years and years I struggled
just to love my life. And then

the butterfly
rose, weightless, in the wind.
"Don't love your life
too much," it said,

and vanished
into the world.
            – Mary Oliver, *One or Two Things*

I

GATHERING THE SKAGIT

SKAGIT: (ska' jit) n. 1. A Northwest Indian word for the river which flows from Manning Park, British Columbia, through western Washington State and out Skagit Bay into the Puget Sound. The Skagit river is known for its annual, and sometimes severe, flooding of the surrounding valley. 2. The fertile valley surrounding the Skagit river. The Skagit Valley is one of the richest farming areas in the world, providing 85% of the world's beet and spinach seed and 50% of the world's cabbage seed.

THE ABALONE DIVES

He'd row while I gripped the sides,
head tipped back by the bulked collar
of the life preserver, eyes dazzled by the light.
And then he'd disappear.

Over there, over
the edge. I'd hold on with both hands
staring at where he'd been,
a flip of sea closing over his fins.

When I'd lost all hope,
that was when he'd surface. Drop
his catch in the bottom
of the boat, abalone and dungeness.

At home we'd steam their shells in butter,
chew their string bands.
The abalone pearls
were mine to keep, though

Such rough teeth were not the pearls
of my imagination.
But I believed in the abalone shells
paved with opal,

Luminescent
under the meat. After the feast
he threw the shells on the driveway,
and in secret I hid them under my bed

Until the stink revealed my theft.
He promised to let me keep my treasure
if I'd keep quiet about the abalone dives.
Why can't I tell my mother? I whined

But there was no answer,
except that he wanted me as sole and silent
witness when he went down. *Trust me,*
he said, *I'll always*

Come back up. And I'll bring you
abalone and moonsnails,
I'll show you the simple stomach
of the sea cucumber.

This is how love was taught:
a bribe, a sudden absence
and the salt muscle reward for silence
on my tongue.

THE MIMOSA ABATTOIR

On the south slope behind the mimosa
my mother slaughtered animals.
The back of a cleaver
was for rabbits, an axe and chopping block
for poultry. Only goats
called for my father
and a gun
because they screamed
and struggled under the knife,
rolling their amber eyes.

On those days my mother
sharpened her own knives,
did her work among the flapping
mess of chickens, split
rabbits bleeding out
on her knees, blue guts
clotting the raspberry canes.
Her lips a martyr's line
as she stretched each rabbit skin to dry,
certain we needed protein.

Although it was forbidden,
I sang to the animals
and gave them names.
Dinner was an unhappy hour,
me sullenly pushing backs
and breasts across my plate.
The appetite later on,
the empty hutch,
barred fridge.

Impossible to act like anything but country
when I brought a town girl home
and introduced her to a sink
of skinned rabbits,
their startled fish eyes
fixed on us.

My dreams were of bologna
pink and processed, the smooth
innocent geometry of circle and square.
I hoarded my quarters
for the school cafeteria, I
hosted secret festivals
of anonymous meat.

There was no predicting slaughter days.
I'd come home and pass my mother
who waved the cleaver grimly at me
from behind the mimosas,
while blood disgorged its salt
into my throat.

THE TRAILER

The year she left my father,
the house and all the cats behind
she bought us a trailer on credit.
We slept on the kitchen table
that was also the bed. Each night
my mother checked the air vents
and wrapped herself around my back.

Those were quiet nights, no
one broke anything. I slept well
on the hard bed, happy
despite the way my mother sat
all day in her white nightgown
looking past me. In the morning
before she was full awake
I would brush her hair, curl
its gloss around my cold fingers.

The first time my mother
brought someone home with her,
I slept on the floor,
marking every breath and gasp
from the tabletop, falling asleep
with my fingers in my ears. Next morning
following so close behind her
when she turned she struck me
with the milk carton, a white splash
on my bare legs. While she dried me

with a towel, he gathered her hair
in his hands, pouring its length
down her back and she
leaned into him and closed her eyes.

At that moment
I struck past them, knocked
a splash of salt across the table, slapped
through the screen door
as my mother called my name.

She didn't come after me.
It was easy for me
to climb to the roof of the trailer
and play my harmonica in the air vents
while they were making love,
my mother crying out her mouths
of loss and he answering
like he knew her, like he'd come from
that place she travelled to
when she drifted past me
all those afternoons
when it was just her
sitting in her nightgown
and just me in a t-shirt
crayoning on the table
that was also the bed.

I

My mother's had three husbands
and three abortions since I've known her.
Her orchids were strings of canaries
soaring over clay pots,
her daffodils
a swarm of yellow butterflies
under the alders.

In the rare darkness of morning
snowstorm, the power out,
my mother came for me.
Wrapped me in her coat
and carried me to a car
clogged with orchids.
Drove me and her pollen-dripping cups
to a heated motel.
We spent the night
under blue tongues, slippers
of flame.

Each spring the Skagit flooded
and she drove us to the tulip festival.
This is how I marked time.
Rows and rows of split mouths
red as the lipstick I rolled across
my lips in the backseat,
lifting my hips
to use the rearview mirror.

By fifteen I had worn paper gowns
in three white rooms.
Three abortions I never had,
though I swear I felt them knocking
in my tight belly.

And my mother's absences.
The way she left me alone
for an afternoon
and I waited
behind the alders.

II

I was seven and should have been elsewhere
when she broke the news
to her third husband. He looked around
the house he'd built
with the poverty of his own hands,
a property now overgrown
with roses. His hands empty
on his thighs and the look in his eyes
Protect me from this.

That spring I learned about strawberries,
how they send out runners to reproduce.
This is what my mother did.
I am simply a graft of her, rerooted.

III

And her bouquets!
Jars of yarrow and tansy
gathered for my morning bedside,
pennyroyal mixed in with the sweet peas,
each flower containing secrets
I failed to hear,
each abortion another gift
in the long string of unacknowledged
gifts behind me.

Her visible breath
in the winter car.
The way she pulled over
dusk filling the space between us
and I'd gather her
hair in my hands.

The way I would remember:

Earth rolled back for ploughing.
Darksilver strands of birds
flashing across the road.
My mother's profile
as she drove.
Diners in other towns.

The dim lights, the hung
smoke, my mother's gaze
drifting past the body
of her single daughter
as I ate what was offered
and grew.

Night came on suddenly
at Kate's Cafe. Outside
the river unhinged its jaws
and swallowed the last of the light.

My mother followed it with her eyes:
that numinous riverbandit,
the rising Skagit.

He imagines himself a redwood.
His wife, arbutus. Daughter a lemon aspen.
Caught in shipyard dreams,
confusion is the clearest emotion
he can name. He watches his daughter
climb the scaffolds of his boats
with the same caution
she climbs his knees at night.
He offers her his hand
to take like a mallet
between her hands
and with her first teeth
bite the callouses
from his palm.

He spends days steaming
and coercing beams
to the right curve.
Cursing, knocking
each nail into place.
In the afternoon
he hears his daughter screaming,
forces her face to his knee.

Her careless braids
snagged by the glue stick,
he bends her neck
and shears close to the skull.
In his hands he holds
the sticky woven branches
of his daughter's first hair.
Her skull visible
under the golden sheen
as he releases her, lighter
than she's been since birth.

In the house, her mother packs.
Because he lives for the hot glue
and tar hiss of his ships
he is not the man she married.
Also he's sleeping with a girl runaway
who could be their daughter.
She says he makes women like boats,
he makes them hollow.

He picks up the plane
and finds it bound to his skin
from his daughter's recent braids.

He selects a rib board
and begins planing. Fragrant loops
of cedar fall from under
his hands. Her braids
gleam on the scrap pile,
her gibbous tears
evaporate in the lumber stacks

and the girl he leaves her mother for
sleeps in a converted chicken coop
waiting for his verdict,
waiting to move in. He can't
make up his mind: sometimes
the girl's a wild dogwood,
sometimes a mulberry.

THE BOATBUILDER

He is a man who strangled dogs with his hands.
A man who answered every salty note
from my mother. A grasping man
who taught me to climb the scaffolds of his boats

Without fear. My father, who lifted me
to show me the octopus hauled from the net,
a red mess lurching into the sea
through a hole in the deck smaller than a knot,

Then threw me in to learn to swim. 25 cents to navigate
the flesh ocean of his back, my feet gripping his spine,
balancing, balancing across his body, my fate
to be his ship, launched in the stinging brine

Of his sweat, as I watched his profile contort
and learned to dance for money, and keep my dances short.

WHITE SHIRTS

Before she had lived ten years
with him, her father had taught her archery
and acquainted her with guns.

When her visits were ended
he spent three weeks
curled in his blue sleeping bag

Dreamt of himself, a hawk
frozen under the ice
of a river. This dream

Would soon belong to her, the child
a chip of mirror in his black eyes.
Years ago he put her on his shoulders

And walked across the acres of his land.
With a roughened hand he turned her face
to the orchard.

Pointed out the single cherry tree
as a gift for her, knowledge of
this catch of white blossoms

Against the white sky. From his shoulders
she was the first to see his mistake.
Just some white shirts

Full of holes
hung on a green line
blowing.

FARM SONG

The April hills are hung with alder breath.
Among the Sitka Spruce, each bare-limbed mauve
breath mingles with my mother's breath.

She starts before it's light. She does not rest,
working to keep pace with those swelling groves,
those April hills all hung with alder breath.

The farm dog follows, nipping at her dress.
Flatulent cows shift, steaming at the trough.
Their wet sighs mingle with my mother's breath.

She kicks the top clean off a deer mouse nest.
The dog whines for the mice cupped in her glove
While April hills are smudged with alder breath.

She tosses naked mice into his mouth.
On two legs he catches them in joyous gulps. His ropes
of panting slaver fog and mingle with my mother's breath

As both her hands vacate the broken nest.
Each mouse is blindly swallowed, sacrificed for bulbs.
Each April hill is hung with this: bereft
mauve alders, ghosts of pollen, mingled with all mother's breath.

The only place I can put their names
together is in this poem. The two
who made me went to court
to renounce all claims
to that relationship.
To catch a glimpse of the other
in my gestures or profiles
was sabotage.

When I came for visits,
my mother stayed in the idling car
fluffing her hair
while I ran in. My father waited
on his porch, sucking his pipe,
finally standing up to take my bag.

What did you imagine?
I asked him once.
Not you, he said, breathing smoke.
I never imagined you.

When did you stop loving him?
I demanded on the drive back,
my shoes marking up the dashboard
until the stern intervention
of her hand.
*Never. I just grew to hate him
more.*

These are the questions
that taught me,
tucked me in at night:
which side are you on?
and *who do you think you are?*

I am theirs. I carry
a blood burden.
The sole witness
to their slim, unrecorded
act of love.

It is not hard to picture my bad sister
fucking the boy she wants to marry. At night
I can hear them crying out
against the stillness of my father's house
as I turn and turn on the narrow couch.
The slap of flesh behind one wall,
and behind the other,
the fierce regulated breath
of my father, my stepmother's careful cough.
We are all awake for this symphony, my father
thinking of the sons he never had.

The whole family waits, eyes straining
against the dark, listening
to my sister who takes her time
coming. My father's fist hits the wall,
there is a noise, but my bad sister
keeps singing.

Alone in the dark
I want to tell her:
I have kept every memory
you have forgotten. I recall
your first boy, the way
he marked your neck with rich plums,
as though he had spent the night
pressing his thumbs to your throat.

And I will remember
this night, too. When you marry
I will remind you
of the way you used to sing
at family reunions, all of us awake
in the dark, listening. The way
we used to wait
in the dark auditorium
for you to come on stage
and dance in your pink slippers,
the way the soles of our feet
ached for you.

This is the future
you insisted would be yours,
despite your childhood
in the uncertain care of your mother
and various men,
the leaky outback trailers
the constant rain.

Defiance is your backbone,
femininity your small hands,
each nail a cultivated pearl,
my half sister with all her hard-won
treasure. Your mother and mine both
loved that same harsh man
we spent our girlhoods escaping

And returning to. Our conceptions
months apart, I guard the past
you can't recall:
you at four in the back room
lifting your blue dress
to cover your eyes
as your mother and another man
coupled on the fire escape.

Perhaps it was that afternoon
hearing your mother
articulate her poverty,
salt of her want filling the air,
that you began to plan your escape.

You have succeeded remarkably well.
Your husband locks a fine gold chain
around your neck.
You spend your days waiting
to feel that heartbeat
taking shape beneath yours.

In the order of your created house
your eyes shine. Polished silver
on the table reflects your buckled
distorted lips. No longer hungry,
or even afraid of hunger,
you sing to yourself as you clean.
The rest of your life
is only a matter of time.

My father was the only one
who saw her go under.
The lifeguard was preoccupied with boys
on the raft, her father was
swimming laps, and I was learning
to put my face under water
with my eyes open.

Without a breath or stirring
the girl slipped off her kickboard.
My father filled his lungs
and followed. Caught her
before the bottom did
and drew her up in his arms, his arms

remembering an evening last August,
diving into the Shire spring
to search for the child
who tired of playing with me,
and left us all. The way he propelled her
through dark water
filled with toppling globes
of carbon dioxide
leading him to the surface
with her lost in his arms, his arms

that never forgot the weight of her
as he passed her to her mother
and the ambulance lights began to swing
up the island road.

This time he claimed the child
first. He brought her
to the surface, a sputtering gift
in his arms, his unburdened arms.

While the lifeguard examined her,
her father cried against her legs,
his breastbone staggering
like a billows.
My father opened his arms
to him. The two men embraced, carefully
keeping their wet hips separate

and from the shallow end
my chlorine-bleary eyes threw rainbows
around the whole scene, until finally, alone,
I dared to go under,
I opened my eyes.

ALLEGRA'S SONG

I

Gordon's farm was too many boys
and too much slaughtering, too many whining blue-
bottles, a sloe-eyed, joyless wife
with too many coiled braids

and too much bosom.
There were always too many chickens
liming the porch, there was always Allegra, furious
in the kitchen, shoving her own bloody

hamburger into the meat grinder over
the sink. My father and Gordon cracked
jokes and walnuts for too many
afternoons, stirring

honey from the honeypull
into their chipped cups. *Honey*
was what Gordon called me too
when I hung around the door,

the girl Allegra never bore.
I was frightened by the attic
where their rough boys
tortured each other with clothespins,

afraid to follow them to the barns
where they branded and gelded
and broke in Percherons
with feet as broad as dinner plates, enormous

frightened yearlings who threatened
with the whites of things: teeth, eyes,
their pale bellies when they reared.
My boys bother you, honey? They'll get the strap,

but I always shook my head no,
letting them go on
with their business: whip and harness,
oldest over youngest.

11

When twilight came, when the deer appeared
in the meadows, sudden as breath,
the boys appeared too, loose-limbed,
balancing the long guns.

I stayed in with Allegra
and patted fresh meat into dinner balls
while rifles burst from the porch,
an explosion

of chickens cluttered the sky.
The boys were off then, downmeadow,
the men following
in a truck full of blades.

Without a glance my way,
Allegra thrust her bare black soles
into Gordon's gumboots.
Time to bring in the horses,

she said. *You watch the meat,*
and the darkness grew dusty as a moth
in my mouth as I sat in the sour
kitchen and quietly stole their honey.

A scream broke that thick sticky silence.
More screams climbed the porch, spilled under the screen door –
I choked. I thought, *this is how*
a deer gets shot. And stopped my ears.

III

The door burst in, Allegra stumbled,
the boys leaping around her like hounds,
Gordon beating them back
with a bloodstained hand

and from her shoulder poured blood
and more blood – her dress roiled with it.
You shot her! My newborn, unfamiliar cry:
You shot her!

Shut up, honey, soothed Gordon,
she had her monthlies,
that sonovawhore stud bit her.
Didn't you hear her screaming? my father asked

Why didn't you let her in?
And I couldn't
answer, my fist with the honeyspool
mired in its amber prison.

Allegra listed in the chair,
the colour leached from her face
and then, looking right at me,
she removed the protective hand

and drew me in. Her wound
was a hinged door she opened for me.
She offered up the flayed depths of her shoulder
where the Percheron's teeth had touched

bone, and the deepest core
was pure white. She had eyes for me alone,
then, the girl she never bore.
Pupils dark and dilated as a deer's

and her look was flush and secret
as blood: *Get out of here.*
This is the last time
I'll tell you. Get out of here.

My father moves us down the track.
I grip the sides of the car
and feel the dark in my mouth, the hollow drop
of mineshafts, echoes of mineral and water.
My father whistles, he knows how to follow
the track with his bare hands,
accepts the limits of sight, the small
circumference of light from his hardhat
piercing the constant night.
But I am a child descending a mineshaft
and my eyes are aching
for even a little
light, so hungry they conjure
colours into the dark,
rings of gold and
indigo.

Learning that light is no promise
of safety does not make me trust
darkness. Outside in the bright
far north summer is a miner who says he loves me.
Weeks ago he took a slim copper pipe
and shaped it into a bracelet I still wear.
All summer his gift turns the sun against me,
throws light in my eyes. His blowtorch
a fierce blue flame. He tells me
not to look or I'll go blind
and while I look the other way

his hand makes shadows
between my legs. I turn to the light
and sparks fly as he welds metal
with one hand and handles me
with the other, and I do not
go blind, there are certain
kinds of light
to which I must be
immune.

Two hundred feet down, enclosed by stalactites,
I press both fists against my eyes
to make my own light.
My need unspoken:
to catch my father's calloused hands
and ask him to keep me
in these chaste caves
where the way is barred
by blue teeth
growing
down the
walls.

MOTHERS & DAUGHTERS

I

She was six (her mother
chopping onions in the kitchen)
the first time he pulled her to his lap
one hand threatening her nape.

When they were alone he would lock the door
lift her and take her nipples
like pink beads between his fingers
the pulse of sperm across her knees.

When she married her uncle came to see her.
She locked her infant daughter in the closet
turned up the radio. The whole visit
her hands like two fish

Netted and struggling in her lap, tugging
and tugging at her skirt, trying
to make talk above the music
and the screams.

II

When I came home
my mother said nothing about the time.
My mother said nothing.

III

When she speaks of herself it is as though
she were someone else, as though the breasts
she cups and places in her bra each morning
were not her own, as though the daughter
she rocks had never been carried
in her quiet body.

As though she were barely acquainted
with that six year old
pissing on her uncle's hand
in her panties, crying with the shame.

Think of the gift
refused, the way she turned her back
on whatever he held in his hands.

IV

Think of the party we could have
me and the three girls who testified
against him. And his two daughters
and his wife, who left town
the night she found their three year old
pinned like a moth on his hand.

37

A theme party, a reunion. We'll make
small talk, gossip on what we wore
the first time, where we were caught.
We'll play pin the mouth on the girl
pin the hand on the mouth
pin the girl on the wall.

I speak of him like a lover.
We met when I was eleven. A blowtorch
was roaring in one hand, welding copper
while the other shuffled through
my underwear. His hands broad enough
to handle me and the blowtorch
at the same time.

(The blowtorch is more than a metaphor. It is more
than a symbol. We were in his workshop. He said
I would go blind
if I looked at the blue flame. I tried
to go blind)

V

Her mind worries these memories as the tongue
which cannot ignore the cut mouth.
She dreams of her daughter growing,
hipbones visible as two handles
on a child's cup. She dreams with the ache of a mother
who longs to press a daughter's ribcage
into permanence, the ache a mother feels
when, despite everything, her daughter's
sex swells.

The way a mother defines safety
as a locked door, the key secure
in her fist.

V I

My mother with her hands twisted in her lap
told me of a woman she knew, raped by three men
in seven months. This woman knew she had no luck,
tried to kill herself by jumping off a bridge.
But she couldn't get the impact right.
She broke almost every bone
and lived. They repaired her body with pins
but could do nothing for the smashed face,
the force of the water that twisted her
into a Picasso woman, one eye smaller
than the other, cheekbones floating
like two broken wings
at the edges of her face.

When she left the hospital
to finish her life
her hands kept floating up
to cover the new image
of her face, blurred like a fetus
dragged unsuspecting into the world.
A wet photograph
jiggled in the light.

Some of us want to be marked that way,
the confession in our bones.

FISHTOWN

These are damp years.
Years of smoke
in your eyes, evidence
of mice in the cupboards
and the blankets on the floor moulding
along with your clothes
add up to one undeniable truth:
If you raise kids in Fishtown
they'll never forgive you.

Sure you don't wallop them
for fingering themselves
as they stand bare-assed
near a fire which puts out
scant warmth. Didn't you
yesterday bring home
a man, or a woman,
and spend the night panting
and thrusting in the dog dark?

Choosing not to see the kid
awake and beady-eyed
listening to the chorus
of you and the mice
and the water dripping
from the roof to the bucket
on the tin-can table.

You may protest
you are following the long
and celebrated tradition
of poets who live
at the perilous edge
of the river
and write poems
about the river's edge.

But your kids don't care
for protest. They want
escape. They either grow to resent you
and continue to live with you
in your dank shack,
becoming just like you
but without the choice
or they turn from you

and become the children
of your nightmares,
the Republican brats. Your son
sporting a military cut
leaves his Bible
casually open to the parable
of the prodigal son
and he means *you*!
His football helmet
rolling like a bomb
near your rancid bed.

You pass your daughter
walking the wet boardway home from school
as you drift downriver in your canoe
to pick up your dope.
Her arms locked
around her purple cheerleading uniform
wrapped in cellophane
to protect it from the mud.

The cellophane blows
wildly, catching the thin
Fishtown sun,
your daughter's home perm
also wild and shining,
the fierce look in her eyes:

this is my way out of here.

II

FORGIVING THE RIVER

for Mami Nomura

Others may forget you, but not I.
I am haunted by your beautiful ghost.

– The Empress Yamatohime

Hito wa isa
Omoi yamu tomo
Tama kazura
Kage ni mie tsutsu
Wasuraenu ka mo

– translated by
* Kenneth Rexroth*

LETTER HOME

Each paper room glows, an egg
cupped to the light.
The house steams: bamboo, green
tea, and outside the river plants
rotting in the sun. Daily
I follow the river to market
to buy figs that will spin blue threads
and spawn gnats by twilight.

Everything is starting to decay.
I can't take this much fertility
alone.

At dawn my landlady bowed at my doorway
and offered a basket of duck eggs
smooth as river stones.
Cracking them over flame
I find her gift is double-yolked
each golden orb
quickening, flecked with blood.

I haven't used my language
since you were here. The nights
your hands walked over my hips
and spoke of rooms
that opened one

into the next, as a string
of red lanterns knock sides
in a storm.
My house is fragile as a blown
egg. The rains
knock the windows loose

in their panes, the cats scream
outside the balsam walls.
If only someone would touch me.

But I can't offer myself
as anyone's anchor
while the river slips past
and carries things away:
stray cats, bicycles, whole trees
tugged from the slopes.

I had to write you now
before the river rises any higher
and pulls me out from under my low blue roof
as a crane plucks an escargot
from its spiraled shell.
I can't speak
the language.

Even if someone
sees me drifting past
I will not be real.
The sun will glance off the water
like I wasn't there. Anyone
will look away from so much light,
turn back to the bowl of green tea
steaming between their hands.

We heard they would jump from buildings
at the slightest provocation: low marks

On an exam, a lovers' spat
or an excess of shame.

We heard they were incited by shame,
not guilt. That they

Loved all things American.
Mistrusted anything foreign.

We heard their men liked to buy
schoolgirls' underwear

And their women
did not experience menopause or other

Western hysterias. We heard
they still preferred to breastfeed,

Carry handkerchiefs, ride bicycles
and dress their young like Victorian

Pupils. We heard that theirs
was a feminine culture. We heard

Even the dawn is thick with heat
in this country. I take my tea out back
to sit by the river,
and find the river has been stolen
in the night. Only a few pools,
a few fish gasping in the mud,
an old man with a net.
Sliding across the rocks, he gleans fish
for the deep basket on his back.
Grey birds scatter.

Behind him a whole crew of workers
pull a wagon piled with bicycles
abandoned to the river, wheels twisted
and clogged with weeds.
The women pulling the wagon
wear sunbonnets under their hardhats.
They work slowly in the heat,
scraping the moss from each rock wall.
I pour the last of my tea on the drying rocks,
go back inside. For weeks I drink my tea
beside the window, staring at a dry ditch
filled with the clang of metal.

That theirs was an example of extreme
patriarchy. That rape

Didn't exist on these islands. We heard
their marriages were arranged, that

They didn't believe in love. We heard
they were experts in this art above all others.

That frequent earthquakes inspired insecurity
and lack of faith. That they had no sense of irony.

We heard even faith was an American invention.
We heard they were just like us under the skin.

Perhaps they heard we don't understand them
very well. Perhaps this made them

Pleased. Perhaps they heard we shoot
Japanese students who ring the wrong

Bell at Hallowe'en. That we shoot
at the slightest provocation: a low mark

On an exam, a lovers' spat, an excess
of guilt. Perhaps they wondered

If it was guilt we felt at the sight of that student
bleeding out among our lawn flamingos,

Or something recognizable to them,
something like grief. Perhaps

They heard that our culture
has its roots in desperate immigration

And lone men. Perhaps they observed
our skill at raising serial killers,

That we value good teeth above
good minds and have no festivals

To remember the dead. Perhaps they heard
that our grey lakes are deep enough to swallow cities,

That our landscape is vast wheat and loneliness.
Perhaps they ask themselves if, when grief

Wraps its wet arms around Montana, we would not prefer
the community of archipelagos

Upon which persimmons are harvested
and black fingers of rock uncurl their digits

In the mist. Perhaps their abacus echoes
the shape that grief takes,

One island
bleeding into the next,

And for us grief is an endless cornfield,
silken and ripe with poison.

The morning they turn the river back on
I am also unprepared. I pull on a robe
and run to the water. So grateful
to have the river back
I forgive the deception, the manmade reality
of its flow. Just as I forgave you your deceptions
when you opened the door
and entered. The way your two hands reclaimed me,
fierce crabs scraping across the riverbottom of my body
as though you had always been there, as though
you had never left.

A N K L E

"Ankle found in Tokyo Park"

– Yomiuri Times, 1994

Separated from foot and calf, no more
than a small reminder. Simply
an ankle
wrapped in plastic, later
sexed female.

Under the Japanese maples
the facts are precise:
this slice was found
at the roots, a cold and dangerous
mushroom.

You may have wanted me
to take a woman's ankle
and create a history for you.

Ask certain questions
about ankle bracelets
and bone structure, missing lovers
and the potential arch
of a foot.

But this slice of her
remains anonymous
as rib-eye steak.

We are left
with the evidence:

a park in Tokyo
in the June season of rain.
Ponds of golden koi,
slow mandarin ducks
and couples with umbrellas.

The maintenance worker
prods the meat disc
from under the maples
with her garbage spear

As somewhere else
a kyuudo arrow
scars the wet air
in its path, piercing
the bull's-eye.

ENGLISH LESSONS FOR EXPATRIATES*

A

When I'm lonely in this country
I go to the market
and read the clothes:

The princess is running in the forest.
It is dark and she is afraid.
Come hither! Come hither! Come hither!
Quite happy.

I spend three days
in the sweater shop
thinking it over, this new &
abridged translation.

B

A flock of schoolgirls pass me on bicycles,
schoolbags strapped to their backs.
I read a knapsack, *Too Drunk To Fuck*
and sink my teeth in my lip

To stifle laughter.
Here my English
is simply garnish.

* all italics are direct quotations from items seen and/or purchased
  while living in Japan.

58

C

Obaasan is oblivious
and her gnarled hands tremble
on the daikon stand.
But I would let her know

That *Another Nigger On The Woodpile*
is not the t-shirt's answer
to the *I Have A Dream* apron
And the combination does not reveal

Which side she is on.
I wanted to travel far from home.
But my language has followed me here,
my language has grown perverse.

D

The stories told here are
the same stories
as where I come from.

But the audience
Is innocent. The audience is a billboard.
INFINITELY. PALPITATE!

Demands the sign
at the border to Takesaki.
I am the only one
who sees my language burning,
Who notices the theatre going up in smoke.

If I knew who wrote this English
I would know
how to address this poem.
And if I could escape narrative

Shame I wouldn't be in Maebashi
drinking *Yop*, drinking *Calpis*,
ignoring each flattering prayer for purchase:
Enjoy The Caucasian Taste!

I wouldn't be here, casually setting
the merchandise on fire
with my *Peace* cigarette lighter,
watching the t-shirts go up in smoke:
Mummy, What's a Sex Pistol?
What's Your Target, This or That?

The skin cup of my hands
brings you water. You drink
and turn away, your mouth
still wet. I catch myself in the mirror
following the cool drift
of your shoulders
down the hall. How I would drink
you! Swallow your history,
the first woman
who wet your skin, your first betrayal
and what you have become,
a parched woman.

Each night I evaporate
a little more against you,
you with your darkdrunk eyes
dragging your tongue
up the anchor of my spine.

Tonight I beak the octopus
with my Japanese knife.
I slice the purple fronds from the legs,
pour the marinade of sesame and sake.
I dig out its hooked mouth
for your pleasure

and dream of us in a wild place
and you in need of water:
How I'd walk miles with my throat full.
How I wouldn't swallow even if I
stumbled. How I'd be a faithful
carrier and always return from the river
to you under the bottlebrush trees,
the mockingbird song
pouring over us. How
I'd empty my mouth
into your mouth. Love,
I'd bring you water.

Tonight I ache: lust settles low,
hooks my spine, burning hot
as sake. You knock entrance,
I offer blood. *What is love*
mocks your mouth,
but a red octopus
twisting &
sucking at the hips?

HAIKU OF THE LOST ARROW

Bows rise in their arms
slow as smoke from blue incense.
The plucked sinews are

partridges whirring
into a bamboo dawn – gone
quicker than breath leaves

a body. Between the
dojo and the targets, tall grass
bends with August heat

while red dragonflies
dance. Sensei is an old woman
whose face is creased as

a bride's kimono –
peach silk wrapped in boxes for
long silent seasons.

Her arrows are good
children coming home from school.
They never wander.

When she has finished
shooting, she claps her hands and
sends me to collect

her arrows from the straw
targets. On the tip of her
morning's last arrow

is a catch of red
lace, pierced wing of a dragonfly.
The body is nowhere

and the wing blows off
like a leaf. I think of you, the mark
you left on me. Not visible

yet tough as morning
spiderweb across the landscape
of my face. They say

I will get past this
but autumn came early
this year, nights of frost even

as summer still burns us.
Now ropes of orange persimmons
hang drying at every door.

Mockingbirds gather
on the rooftops while dogs snarl,
chained to the walls.

I bow and hand Sensei
her arrows. All but one that
I can't find, though

I combed the long grass
with my fingers. One arrow
gone. Perhaps underground

you hold it in your hand
against the broken dawn. You
are the wandering

arrow, the bow unstrung.
Your sudden absence has startled
the partridges from the plums.

THE MAGICIAN

All I can come back to is the river
the way I ran to it
each night after your death
the way I crept through its shallows
and felt the tug of deeper water.

Each night I followed the river
until I reached the end of the shore,
the place where the white cranes
spend the night. When they saw me coming
they lifted the iridescent tubes
of their necks, opened their wings
and spread themselves against the dark.
Bats swooped. The air shook with life.

When my knee shattered one night
as I leapt the wet stones
and slipped
there was peace in that, too,
the way I collapsed back to earth
both hands on the ground
beneath me.

Nobody knows how I made it home.
The truth is, I felt no pain.
Those white cranes lifted on the night air
and flew over me.
Drops of riverwater
fell from their black feet
and pain vanished.

I dragged my leg across the rocks,
I walked miles in the night.
It was some kind of magic,
but nothing compared to
your sleight of hand,
your disappearance.

COMFORT

Some nights even the river doesn't comfort.
Some nights the cats just won't stop crying,
the cicadas an electric whine
strung against the dark. The road to the river
is smeared with butterflies,
their wings gleam in the moonlight.
At the edge of the river
the orange cats sing to me
their mouths split to a howl of white
teeth as they are entered.

It's been weeks since I've come here.
I've stopped seeing you
riding through the streets on your bicycle
your black hair streamed by the wind
as riverweeds ride the tug of the river.
I am no longer tricked
into following girls with hair like yours
thinking it might be you
turning the corner
slipping past me.

This summer I burned
a fistful of blue incense
at your grave, stirred the ash
of your bones with a long stick, poured
water on the chaff of your hair
and the night was a cat with torn ears
moaning around the corners of my house.

It's autumn now. Pomegranates
split themselves
on the trees. Each breath
hangs in the air
fragile as the white cranes
spread against the night. The cats
know it too, this is what
they cry out against
as they arch their spines
to the dark:

>   the night encroaching,
>   the constant return to the river.

When you touch your mouth to my closed eyes
I want to tell you I am still dreaming
of low-slung Japanese roofs, persimmons rolling
into the scented gutters, the face of a woman
I never touched, the mouth
of a woman whose heart stopped
a month to the minute you came to my bed.

I touch the bone necklace under your breasts
and feel your breasts catch my palms.
In that riotous motion, I catch her moving past me
as I have seen her every day since she left,
her profile as she turns a corner, that breath
of recognition as I find her leaving

And leaving again, as though
she'd come back to memorize this town
to verify each stretch of still water
that blankets the rice fields
and reflects the oyster coloured sky
before travelling.

Your hands trek down the slopes of my back,
your mouth sings over my scars
and I hear her mother calling
in a voice as flat as a summer river
*Daughter, why don't you rise? Everyone
has come for you.*

Birds in the river trees sing in the thousands,
the sound of rainsticks
poured and poured outside every window
of my house. The way I turn my back on a woman
unbinding her coils of blueblack hair
who takes her time
leaving our bed, the way I move into
the open mouth of what you have to offer
the catch of your breath that promises:

> *this is only the beginning*
> *of what could happen to us.*

III

OPENING THE STORM EYE

AUBADE

Consciousness is a gift brought by the dawn.
They watch her crawl across the floor
and locate each item of clothing. Her silver chains
are lost, all her rings are gone.
They won't meet her eyes, bashful boys now,
dust cracking lips in the dry air.

The sand leaves a trail
from where they picked her up on shore,
the girl left behind
at the high school bonfire.

From what has fallen out of her
you could find your way back to the sea:
pliant mute, pliant mermaid, each step
a blade entering. Love's cost.
Woken briefly by the grinding in and out of her.
Sand in her mouth and falling from her skin
as she tried to push it away.
But it drove in.

Beauty, she slept on bare wood
and her dreams were blunt with alcohol.
And it is no surprise this morning
when one of them offers to drive her home
as if she'd had a flat on the highway
and they'd pulled up behind her with a jack.
As if she'd been rescued by them.
She resists the urge to thank them
or breathe too hard their smell on her skin.

Aurora now, one of them opens the cabin door
onto a mess of sunlight and purple alders.
Her heart jolts as they pass around
morning's whisky. Something pricks her finger.
She has misplaced all three wishes,
can not think of the end of the story.
And her hands are burned from where, they said,
she caught fire.

Someone put her out.
Alcohol is ether
and she is full of unconscious
grace. He leads her to his truck,
opens the door for her.
At the bottom of her driveway
he drops her off, spitting
gravel as he leaves,
and she hurries home
missing a sandal,
bends at the door to slip off its mate.

LARKSPUR

for Ellen

He wore a low hat. He had an irregular gait.
You were moving boxes from the elevator.
He left you on the floor, fingermarks on your throat.

The door was left ajar. He forced your legs apart.
You'd planned to put windowboxes over the radiator.
He wore a low hat. He had an irregular gait.

You'd never seen him before, wearing his suede coat.
You'd moved to Brooklyn seven months before
he left you on the floor, fingermarks on your throat.

The evidence was intact. You were his scapegoat.
Your family was called to the Emergency Ward.
You whispered: handgun. low hat. couldn't run. irregular gait.

Your mother held your hands. Your father held your feet.
Your parents drove you home and locked their door.
In nightmares he rides you to the floor, fingers around your throat.

Anniversary: no tears. Your mother takes you to the Ritz
While your father fills your rooms with purple Larkspur,
Sunflowers. Who wore a low hat? Who had an irregular gait?
Who walked out, was never caught? Your fingers recall your throat.

You spin the wheels of your red truck
and speak of tornados you've known
how they drive through homes
and create orphans.

I see your girlhood divided
by unremarkable years
and years where you crouched in the bathtub
and prayed to the deep and steady anchor
of the plumbing
that you would be left alive
after house and family had been sucked away.

Picking out cherries from a roadside stand
unaware of the change in weather,
of you behind me.
As your lips claim my neck
the red relents in my fist. Coins
scatter in the fruit as the sky rolls over us.
The rain comes in sheets
like the wings of netted birds
throbbing and falling.

While I buy the fruit
you wait in your red truck
playing the engine.
I stumble to meet you
drunk on the curve of your mouth,
a cardinal on fermented autumn berries.
With my tongue
I would lick the dust from your eyes,
I would offer shelter.

SETTLEMENT

Under the terms of agreement
you'll keep this city,
I'll find a new one.

I'll keep what I have smuggled
past city limits, the span
and measure of your hand

locked in the lantern of my body,
all your stories, blown
like stained eggs from your lips,

all I have swallowed.

SEVEN MINUTES IN APRIL

Cherry blossoms drifted
from the park to the gutter.
We had no time.
You lay down on a pile of clean laundry
still unfolded on your bed
unbuttoned your jeans
and slid them over your hips
the dish of your pelvis
rising with the motion of undressing.
You were cheating on your new girlfriend
and I was there to help.

Still standing, your mouth on me
I came first, quick as the April rain
rattling the cherry trees.
Stopped for the moment it takes
to draw a full breath
take a stronger hold on your hips
and make circles between us
until we did it again, together, your teeth
closing on the cotton over my nipple.
Seven minutes.

Your orange cat snaked one paw
under the door. For the last time
we disengaged our hands.
I gathered the photographs
for which I'd come
and slipped out the back window
to an alley clogged with petals.

Once two women boiled a chicken
and tore it apart over the pot.
It was a fine chicken.
They ate with their hands, sucked the bones
dry of marrow. *This is how it felt to be Napoleon,*
says one to the other, kissing the poultry juice
from her chin, pulse beating *victory,*
victory.

A woman in a Vancouver asylum weeps
on her psychiatrist's shoulder. *It was me!*
I destroyed the Canadian economy!
she sobs. *Lord Jesus, why didn'tcha protect me*
from the casinos?

The casino is a human abattoir.
Or it is a fine place
for a night on the town.
Welfare cheques are cashed there
and romance jingles between the slot machines.
Gamblers stumble under the lights,
glazed with the sauce
of potential First World wealth.

A woman in a Montreal asylum
clucks on her psychiatrist's shoulder,
pecks at his dandruff with her hard little bill.
She will only take her pills
when the nurses scatter them
on the floor. Grain fed.

Love relies on fine distinctions.
In various economies of the Third World
the red wattles between a girl's legs
are cut with sharp stones. No one cares to admit
an ancestral relationship to poultry.

Here we snip our boys clean. That loose
skin is entirely too much
turkey! Here we gamble
that men will be too drunk
on the possibility of becoming rich
to notice the cockscombs of the female sex
leering at them, uncut.

Listen! she screams
before the needle goes in:
Something is stirring in the trees –

The Wind in the Wattles. Unquote.

SNAKE'S TONGUE

She spoke limited acrid English.
Crouched over my face
and spread bitterness across my palate.
My lips against an expanse of scar
while a flap of her skin
trailed in my mouth, beating
a snake's tongue against my tongue.
As a girl she cut herself there
to stop her sex from unfolding
into something more dangerous
to her father than it already was.
This act was performed
in a foreign country
many years before.

It made me so dizzy,
that long tail of skin
in my throat. Still I kept my mouth
on her despite the scars and bitterness.
This was the best I could do. My hands
held her hips as she rocked
across my face, closed her eyes
and travelled past me.

That night we slept with our fingers cocked
inside each other, that loose tongue
of hers wet against my thigh.
In the morning I was miserable.
Scorched by that severed lip
even through the knife-edged
winter of this country.

What made you? I asked. *You were only eleven.*

She said, *I was through with being a woman.*

THIS SALT

Montreal, 1996

One night in your storm bed
changed me, Isabelle. You cut my tongue
from its hinge, bruised my lips
against the bone of your pubis. I evaporated
against you, touched your sheets with salt.
Your bed a wet song. Our arms slapped the sheets
as the wings of cormorants slap water
before flight. We rose and rose to each other.
And in the morning standing barefoot on your fire escape
above the cloisters and the blue angel of Mont Royal
glinting in the thin sun of April
you stood behind me, opened your kimono
shaped your breasts to my shoulderblades
pressed your mouth to my wet ear.
I leaned over the edge and reached for the angel.
Below us another Easter parade, virgins
lined the sidewalks. Goats' eyes marbled
in the Portuguese shops where they hung.
Help me, you whispered.
Let me keep this salt
on my hands.

IV
GIVING MY BODY
TO SCIENCE

SESTINA OF THE GEOGRAPHIC TONGUE

Geographic Tongue: "One with raised areas due to thickening of
the surface cells, giving the appearance of a map."
                                   – The New American Medical Dictionary

"... outlined by margins in a grey-yellow or whitish, constantly
changing pattern. Also known as fissured tongue, lingua
plicata, or migratory glossitis."
                                   – Dictionary of Medical Syndromes

If I offered you my geographic tongue,
would you be able to tell without speaking:
This is a road map. This is a map home.
Here is where the village river drifted
over my grandmother's bare feet. Here is her street
where the wind dropped bone grit in the throat. Here is the star

with its six points, and here are the stars
sharpening their points against many tongues.
Some drank starlight on these barbed streets.
Some ate grit and clay and died without speaking.
Those who survived were cut loose and drifted
through a strange geography, far from home

and familiar tongues. No, Montreal was never home
to her, just a place to pass dreams to her children: *Star
light, star bright,* and their English was a drift
of snow in the mouth that froze her tongue
and split her apart from them. She made them speak
her errands and was afraid to go alone in the street.

Now my tongue is cobbled like a village street
and the river of her girlhood has finally come home
to sing in my mouth. I know, though my father rarely spoke
of it. I know about the spoiled meat torn like a bloody star
between the village children who died of eating, numb-tongued,
mute. The starlit worksongs that drifted

over the Hungarian fields all the way to Israel, drifted
like a red tide of song, in and out of the oily streets.
Here is her only son speaking a once-dead tongue
and here are the blue-skinned grapes of his new home.
Here are the hops. The same low stars
hang over the kibbutz. Here is her son standing without speaking

and becoming my father. Without speaking
I want you to understand. I am proof of my parents' drifting
love. I am proof of the shawl and the star
that those left behind wore like a caul and a scar through streets
bound in wire. Her memories of home
became a burnt map, a gutted flame, and many tongues

were cut out for speaking. And the streets
were darkened by drifting ash and home
now is just the faint lines of a star etched upon my tongue.

Our bodies are dangerous.
  Each flap, each opening
provokes needles, knives.
  We bring new life forth,
autograph the opus.
  Our children bear
the scars of trust.

foreskins, tender-lipped
  foreskins. yakuza fingers,
stumped yakuza fingers.
  tumorous breasts, stone-
bearing breasts.
  the clitoral cut,
outskirts of women.

Who will claim
  the parts removed?
Are they malignant,
  are they loathed?
Body's link to
  a primitive past:
Or reminder of what has
  returned to ash:

throat cherries plucked:
  tonsillectomy.
vaginal vault:
  hysterectomy.
gut's roadblock:
  appendectomy.
jews' teeth,
  the bones of jewish
  ghettos.

Punishment
  for stealing bread:
The price
  of soldier's swollen blood:
Unsexed
  to keep a virgin pure:
Or silenced
  that they speak no more:

severed hand,
  young thief's hand.
broken membrane,
  enemy membrane.
lovely castrato,
  golden castrato.
prisoners' tongues,
  stained sheet on the door.

THE SHARED HEART

I   BIRTH

A mother is divided by a line
that turns suddenly red
as a papercut and fills with blood.
Two infants with one heart
are exposed to life
without a cry:
their eyes are open,
their arms around each other.

The multi-chambered heart pulses
more and more gently. Two infants
fade to blue
until the entrance of tubes, the plastic
gasp of oxygen.

The new mother feels both lighter
and heavier. She touches the wet bandage
across her belly, turns
toward the machines
that cradle her twins.
She would give her own
oversized heart
for even a chance.

One of them is scheduled to die
in tomorrow's operation.

A surgical team severs the bonds
between them. One twin has no heart
anymore. She dies.
The surgeons can't stop,
too busy trying to save her sister.
In one wet glove, a cardiologist
holds their heart
pumping and gasping, a trout
cut from the riverbed.

A nurse gathers the dead twin
in blankets. Her eyes are open,
her arms reach for what was taken.

Someone slips the heart back
into the blessed girl's
chest cave,
Ah! But this girl
is not made for a whole
heart. She can't straighten
her head. Her hands clutch
the hem of air, looking for
her sister's hands. Her eyes
the bruised indigo of newborns.

Some amputees suffer nostalgic pain
in their missing limbs. This girl
is nothing but ache, nothing but questions
of why she was chosen, why
they were not loved
as they presented.

She grows and her chest scars
shut. She goes painfully to school,
carrying between her breasts
a white storm of scars, as though the heart
is caged in place
only by this net.

Her head always tilted back
to make a place for the absent sister.

When half-grown she takes her first man.
Learns to live for nights on her back,
her head thrown back. A man plunging into her,
touching and touching the hard scars
with his tongue, the raised white
between her nipples.

Her eyes closed. Her arms locked
around him.
Her fingers drum a heartbeat
on a man's smooth back.

APPRENTICESHIP OF THE
PHLEBOTOMIST

The hardest to learn was the standard
blood draw. I had never
entered anyone before
with such a fine point. My palpation
of the softest skin between wrist
and bicep – my aim was flawless,

yet the first kid passed out cold, eyes rolled
back in his head, metallica tattoo
stark on his white arm. *Don't worry*
said the phlebotomist, *it happens,*
these guys are the worst with their own blood.

The phlebotomist who taught me
could draw with a butterfly
from the tiny vein running in the knuckle
or along the scalp of an infant, from a vein
thin as a flax stem, tough as
blue linen threads under the skin. She
was a blood diviner.

Don't look for it, she'd tell me
It's not something you can see. Just let
your fingers tell you where the needle should go.

It was like sewing, but I've always hated sewing.
The precise stitch, the concentration
in the thumbs. Made me want to scream,
all that digging blind under the skin.

That year I learned universal precautions,
how we were supposed to treat everyone
the same, everyone
as contaminated.

That wasn't much help
when I drew my first AIDS blood.
The patient told me how it was. I doubled my gloves.
I had eleven tubes to pull from his veins.
On the fifth tube
he started to run dry. I shook a bit
thinking he would soon die, and
a plum fish opened and closed its mouth
under his skin. Red swam behind my eyes,
arterial blood battered my temples.
Everything became narrow
and bright as needles.

He looked right into me
and saw only fear. *It's okay,*
he soothed me. *Try my other arm,*
there's a good one there.
He talked me through as I drained
what there was in his other vein
and then swabbed and entered
the back of his hand.

No one has ever so opened their heart to me
as that junkie, whose crimson blood
streamed willingly into each tube
which I gathered, after, and held
in both hands, a bunch
of glass tulips.
Thank you, he said, *for being gentle.*
Everyone's afraid –

SMALL JUSTICE

for Tess

He's gone before you,
the one who taught you
what you learned of love.
That's small justice,
cousin, but small coins
might make a dollar
eventually.

You will go before us.
You will drift away
in a sea of night sweats.
Already your body
has become the furnace
of a ship. You burn
through the night
and the sheets
are water.

On this shore we stand
with our foolish confetti
and our white handkerchiefs
waving up a storm. We are
not sure our voices carry

over water. You smile patiently
from where you are, long past
the bitterness that keeps
us here, and our terror
of love's pandemics.

In the toss of waves
your future beckons,
a stolen necklace.
Some crows gather,
attracted by the glitter.
They set up a dark
& raucous debate.
We don't know
if the sound carries
over water.

And finally
there is an absence.
No nipple in your mouth
these apricot nights.
No movement in love
across the living room.

So, you escaped Shoah to be consumed by this. Our last day:
you moaned, the eggs were too wet, their mucous collected
in the corners of your mouth, you turned away from
the amber stink

Of the port-o-let in the corner, asked me to do your nails.
Your socks clung like bark to your swollen feet.
I lifted your edema'd ankles and pared the rinds
from each cool block

In my hands, dry and smooth as madrona. When I finished
your left foot and began to skin the sock off your right,
your breathing changed. Your eyes filmed and startled on my face,
on the generations between us: you did not know me then

But I was granted sudden wisdom. I knew you were dying, called your
children in. Phlegm lifted and bubbled to a cork in your throat.
I'm looking at an angel, said your son, amazed: he put his head
between your breasts and listened.

I didn't want to let you go, Evelyn, wiping and wiping the last
foam from your gummed mouth, the gold froth that rose
and fell with each breath of you. I sat on one side, your son
and his wife on the other, your son not daring

To raise his head. I held your hands and uncurled
your fingers from your palms. What more could you have wanted
as a girl but such a death, at home
with your family and years away from Germany?

Only the last things remained: cleaning your mouth
and lowering your bed so you could rest. I held the control
in my hand and pushed the button to let you down by degrees

And by degrees your son with his face against your heart
descended with you until you were flat as the horizon
and he was a dark mound of shoulders rising from the land
of your body, humming with unnecessary oxygen.

It may be necessary to cause the patient
some discomfort in order to accurately assess
his condition.

Don't be afraid, I know this hurts
says the man in the mask, entering
my esophagus with a long tube
while I make eyes at him. I know this hurts
but we must have balanced amnesia
not the cawing of crows outside,
not the distractions.

The practitioner must be aware of such feelings

I predict exploration followed by
extrusion. A possible ectopia
with consequent loss of blood
& wandering uterus. Grip your bed, my grief
my grand mal, you'll soon be caught
in a glossolaliac haze, you're going under!

The patient usually presents
some degree of anxiety about his illness
or about the examination itself.

He says I'm going down but won't tell me why.
I pray for oblivious health
my mouth in the noose of an O,
I ask for homeostasis and peace.

It is essential to offer a sympathetic response to such
unvoiced apprehensions

Only a little longer, he whispers.
Be patient. Clearly you have another chance
at offspring. It was just the size
of a gilled fish, a gold fish, nothing
that you could actually hold. I need you
to open your legs, he says
placing a basin between them.
Please be a patient.

Schizophrenia is not the sole cause of inconsistent histories

We must have balanced anesthesia. I mean
I just have to get in there, he says
torturing my arm for a better vein. This is not
simple surgery, my sacrum, my serum. I fear
toxemia, I have to be sure.
The tympany of his fingers
on my abdomen.

It is wise to deflect personal inquires
by the patient

I mean, think of me
and my anatomy. While you dream
a ballet of slow water
and koi, I must bring it forth: blood
and amnesia. I need you,
my xiphoid, my zygote,
Don't you agree?

It is useful to begin the interview
with non-directive questions:

What brought you in today?
What did you think we could do?

POSTCALL

Postcall you come home diminished, wan, your hands
faltering at the lock. You need to tell me
each patient's history before you sleep,
the progress of each malignancy, the way the family
spoke to you, the suffering that makes each death a lottery.
I understand. But I wait for you, Isabelle,
not your stories of the progress of the dying.
I lead you to bed like a child, almost crying
with fatigue and despair these anaemic mornings
when you have donated all your strength
and then come home to me, stricken, empty
and grateful for the smallest gesture of tenderness,
my easing your heel from your boot as you undress,
holding you while you try to reclaim your membership
as one who sleeps. Your limbs twitch
like a dog's, hurrying into dreams, your lips
part with breath. I soothe you with my weight,
whisper about the snow piling up outside.
Your eyes close on this slant-shadowed day, blue
repose beckons. But even in sleep
your fingers pleat the quilt
as if gathering the flesh of an arm before a shot.
I understand. Accountability never leaves your hands.

The lungs project above the medial one third
of the clavicle while the skull holds a bone
like a fossilized butterfly. Each cranial nerve
tells its own story and the innominate bones
resemble nothing but themselves –

The throat begins with a trap
door. Liquid has two choices:
esophagus or trachea,
stomach or lungs. Mostly
there is no choice:
the epiglottis
clamps, water
does not enter
the lungs.

Today she drains her first lung. Last night
I held her while she told me so. Today
in her books I find *lung*, I find
the position where her needle will enter –

All winter I have studied
anatomy. Love taught me
to cherish the sponged
bulk of a lung. When
I run my tongue
up the slopes
of her body
I know each
name, each
location:
skin over
manubrium
over lung.
All that I love
is layered.

One night in five I lie alone, she stays
at the hospital. At night comes the firstblown
snow. Yesterday her friend died in childbirth
in Rome. The anesthetic took her under.
Her lungs snagged on a certain breath
in a certain Roman clinic –

It was Sunday, bells were ringing
beyond the olive trees
outside city limits.
Women in black shawls
were already gathered
for bad news. My lover
has confined her grief
to saying, as if in faith
or prayer –

Such things shouldn't happen anymore.

Love, the world
is half in and half out
of your tired hands.
There is a baby
left behind
in a Roman clinic
as yet
innominate.

DELIVERY

While I lay on the rocks, reaching
into the darkness, learning
little by little to love
our only world.

– Mary Oliver

Your plaqued heart has been cheating you
for years, you jerk, you
stutter along, muttering about poverty
the way you've done since I was young
and slushed after you in gumboots
as you scavenged the shoreline.
Dug out barnacles as they hurried to fold up
their oriental fans. Dropped everything raw
and free and gelatinous into my mouth: this sea kelp,
this broken-spined urchin,
while I lay on the rocks, reaching

for the brightest starfish, the small pastas of their legs
sticking to the rock as I tugged them off.
Don't, I screamed as you came with your knife,
I can't, I won't eat it!
You stood over me, that orange star breathing
in my hands, your heart beating
faster and faster just to keep up with me.
How long before your crown arteries
start giving away their gold again?
Your heart's anemones clenching and releasing
into the darkness, learning

to treasure each electric impulse,
to take no chamber for granted.
That day we were out in your dinghy at Grey's Cove
fishing for cod, getting nothing but sea cucumber
and dogfish. The last dog we caught, sluggish
with labour, turgid as a wet leather glove.
You threw her into the bottom of the boat,
keepsake. My job to give her buckets of sea
while you rowed us to shore,
the dogfish opening her body like a cave
little by little to love

out of which nothing came but water.
You put her in the bathtub, turned
the tap on high. She swam. When you left the room
I added shakes of salt
and she bloomed, yes! the bathtub became astonishing
as she spilled a storm-catch of dogfish, each
churning its plums and greens, roiling like kelp-weed,
poisoned by fresh water, already dying,
lurching as your heart does now,
air-hungry, cut-gilled
in this: *our only world.*

GIVING MY BODY TO SCIENCE

I

You think it was easy, deciding to give you my body?
I had first to get over the idea of immortality,
then vanity, and finally, the fear of being laughed at.
But here it is, in writing. Giving
my body is an act of faith
to which you can only aspire,
I've done it.

It is taken for granted in my family
that knowledge
depends on familiarity
with the heart's own weight,
the pleura, all the layers of the eternal cadaver
and a certain irony and a certain reverence.

Take my godgiven eyes, the near and far sighted.
Study iris and retina for clarity
and ask yourselves how I saw the world,
inchoate as a Monet garden. I tell you
I have ached looking across a slow river,
the blue mountains cupping the city
like the shell of a chipped egg.

Touch me like that, with reverence.
Lift up my glands like a rosary.
At night I came home to my lover
who told me of her day at the hospital,
the endless need to suture.
At night I wrapped her body in my arms.
These arms, with their muscles split and spread
for you. I wrapped my leg around her,
pulled her in. This scarred tibia,
the screws still in the bone,
the mystery of steel exposed, flesh rent.
Do you know, can you guess my accident?

II

The truth is, I'm not even fooling myself.
All I have to offer is my body.
My name and history
unknown to you,
that's the only way you'll have me.
Less than meat
in your hands.
I wanted to be divine.
I can't even nourish.

Remember who I was then, clean
as you who snap your gloves
off your perfect fingers, wrap
the plastic over my sections, scrub
your hands free of my stink and walk
from the lab through the winter
afternoon, the pale sky with trees
stark as black coral,
the cold filling your lungs,
keen as the first cut you made along my abdomen.
I gave what I had and now you begin.

Take this love gift: cleft my skin.

ANASTOMOSIS

If we had not spent all this time mouth to mouth
I would not mourn like this, Isabelle
left to myself for a night.
Love between us leaves no space

It leaves no space, we are mouths
upon mouths meeting after the alarm is fumbled
and we struggle apart in the sheets.
What will your day be like?

You ask, as the dog and I walk you to the bus.
I tell you lesson plans, chores and poetry.
How I'd like to show you the hibiscus blooming
but you are home only after dark

When the blue-veined petals have folded
their dusky wings and fallen like moths at first frost,
like the hands of your patients
against the sheets.

Daily you grow more astonished
at the careful rigor of our two bodies,
the way we continue to pulse and desire
independent of light or season.

Coming back alone I clean the house
then rest on the sofa, the dog
curled like a prawn
rising and falling on my bladder.

I read poetry, doze,
push away the hours till morning
when I'm full awake, the day lived without you.
As the atrioventricular arteries arch

Around each chamber of the heart, twist
apart and then anastomose,
so do I always come back to you
and so do you always return to me

Bearing small gifts: winter pomegranates,
fragrant coffee, but also
dark essentials: mouth
to mouth, joined breath.

And in your absence I am no more
than that hibiscus folded in darkness
and no less than that fist of red and pollen
spilt on the cedar floor.

STILL LIFE WITH CLAVICLE

After a day in the emergency room,
our apartment contained a rare silence:
the light across your mouth as you washed me,
the carmine orchid blooming across the wall.
My quiet body was the sweetest miracle, I lay
all evening in devotion, watching over it:
the rich blue IV bruise streaking my arm,
the scaphoid abdomen performing its uneven dance,
the drooling anus learning to sleep again.
Each organ lay listening to the rain,
and it was enough to be still,
without anguish. *Why do we ask for more?*
I asked when you brought me water.
My hands uncertain, I spilled down my neck.
Water pooled in my clavicle. You stirred
this pool with one thin finger,
then bent your head to drink.

"The Trailer" was first published in *Contemporary Verse* 2.

"Opening The Storm Eye" was first published in *Prairie Fire*.

"Forgiving The River" and "Of This More Is Yet To Come" were first published in *Arc*.

"Mothers & Daughters" was first published in *The Fiddlehead*.

"The Performance" was first published in *The Seattle Review*.

"Return to Your Skin" was first published in *Calyx*.

"The Abalone Dives" was first published in *This Magazine*.

"Aubade," "Small Justice," and "One Night In Five," were first published in *The Capilano Review*.

"What We Heard About the Japanese" and "What the Japanese Perhaps Heard" were first published in *Verse*.

"Postcall" was first published in *The Journal of the American Medical Association*, 278, no. 13 (1997): 10587.

"Farm Song" was first published in *Canadian Woman Studies*.

"The Boatbuilder" was first published in *The Antigonish Review*.

"One Night In Five" was first published in *Prism International*.

"Beaking The Octopus" and "Seven Minutes In April" are forthcoming in *Between Our Lips*, edited by Pat Califia.